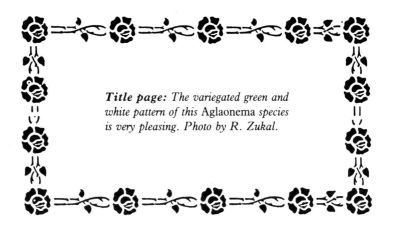

Title page: The variegated green and white pattern of this Aglaonema *species is very pleasing. Photo by R. Zukal.*

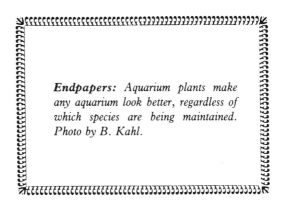

Endpapers: *Aquarium plants make any aquarium look better, regardless of which species are being maintained. Photo by B. Kahl.*

The Beginner's Guide To
AQUARIUM PLANTS

Written By
Dr. Don L. Jacobs

Contents

© 1986 by T.F.H. Publications, Inc. Distributed in the UNITED STATES by T.F.H. Publications, Inc., 211 West Sylvania Avenue, Neptune City, NJ 07753; in CANADA by H & L Pet Supplies Inc., 27 Kingston Crescent, Kitchener, Ontario N2B 2T6; Rolf C. Hagen Ltd., 3225 Sartelon Street, Montreal 382 Quebec; in CANADA to the Book Trade by Macmillan of Canada (A Division of Canada Publishing Corporation), 164 Commander Boulevard, Agincourt, Ontario M1S 3C7; in ENGLAND by T.F.H. Publications Limited, 4 Kier Park, Ascot, Berkshire SL5 7DS; in AUSTRALIA AND THE SOUTH PACIFIC by T.F.H. (Australia) Pty. Ltd., Box 149, Brookvale 2100 N.S.W., Australia; in NEW ZEALAND by Ross Haines & Son, Ltd., 18 Monmouth Street, Grey Lynn, Auckland 2 New Zealand; in SINGAPORE AND MALAYSIA by MPH Distributors (S) Pte., Ltd., 601 Sims Drive, #03/07/21, Singapore 1438; in the PHILIPPINES by Bio-Research, 5 Lippay Street, San Lorenzo Village, Makati Rizal; in SOUTH AFRICA by Multipet Pty. Ltd., 30 Turners Avenue, Durban 4001. Published by T.F.H. Publications, Inc. Manufactured in the United States of America by T.F.H. Publications, Inc.

1.
Why?

The beginning hobbyist presented with the vast array of aquarium plants usually experiences three predictable reactions:

(1) He is delighted with the enchanting new world of underwater gardening to which he has been introduced.

(2) He is bewildered by the number and variety of plants available and wonders how he will learn to distinguish one from the other.

Growing plants well in your aquarium can be as rewarding—and as much fun—as keeping fish. Photo of the popular aquarium plant water sprite by R. Zukal.

(3) He is perhaps a trifle envious of the lovely planted aquariums he has seen and would like to know how to arrange the plants for maximum effect, how to care for them, and how to grow them.

An aquarium without plants, like a home without furniture, is basically livable but ugly, uncomfortable, and inefficient.

Uses of plants

While there has been considerable debate about the necessity for keeping plants in aquariums, there is no doubt that they have many functions. Some of the purposes they serve are:

(1) As natural decorations they are essential to aqua-scaping.

(2) They aid in displaying fishes. Most fishes take on a more intense color, display their finnage better, and court, strut, and behave more normally in a well-planted situation. Different plants can be selected to furnish the most suitable background for each type of fish. Light-colored plants like water sprite and hygrophila offer a dramatic background for black mollies and other dark fishes. Iridescent rasboras, glowlight tetras, neons, and the like take on a richer glow among dark-colored *Cryptocoryne*.

Nothing can beat plants as natural decorations for the aquarium. Photo by A. van den Vieuwenhuizen.

Both floating and rooted plants can provide good shelter and a feeling of security for the fish; shown is Anubias nana. *Photo by Edward C. Taylor.*

(3) They provide shelter for baby fish, shy fish, weaker fish, and females giving birth.

(4) They serve as food for vegetarian fishes.

(5) They help prevent green water by competing with algae for nutrients and serve as a spawning medium for many fishes.

(6) Plants aid in water conditioning by removing nitrogenous wastes, carbon dioxide, and sulphur substances and adding or redistributing oxygen to lower water and gravel areas.

(7) They increase the browsing surface for food produced inside the aquarium. Algae and minute animals such as rotifers, tiny worms, and protozoans, which are eaten by many fishes, may densely cover rockwork, gravel, aquarium walls, and plant leaves. When fish are busy pecking at the leaves they are feasting off these tasty morsels.

Not all are usable
Several tens of thousands different kinds of plants inhabit our globe. A large number of these grow rooted in soil in the warm,

9

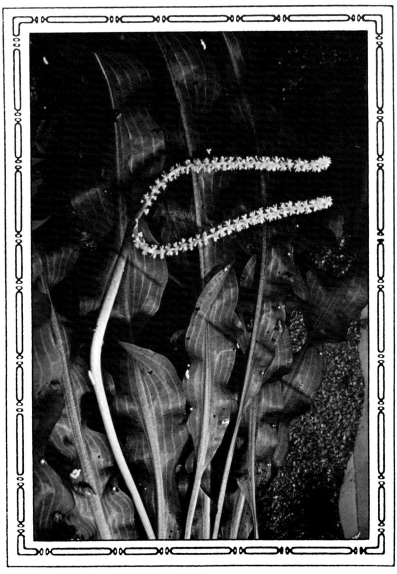

The more densely planted the tank, the greater the degree of shelter provided, obviously—but not every fish does well in a plant-crowded tank. Photo of Aponogeton ulvaceus by T.J. Horeman.

Many fishes regularly pick over the surfaces of leaves of the plants in their tank to obtain added nourishment. Photo by R. Zukal.

moist tropics, but some kinds are found only in deserts, a few in bubbling hot springs, some only on Arctic tundras or on mountain slopes, some on tree trunks, some in the oceans, some in quiet lakes and marshes, and some only in fast flowing streams. Which are usable in aquariums? Many garden plants look as though they would make attractive aquarium plants—but will they grow in the water?

The answer is that about 1,600 different kinds of plants, exclusive of the many kinds of algae (e.g., seaweeds and pond scums), are confirmed water-lovers, but if ordinary land plants are put in an aquarium they will literally drown and rot away.

The list of possible aquarium plants is further cut sharply by the fact that a good many of them grow too large, need too much light, or insist on growing right up out of the water. More than 500 different plants have been discussed in aquarium books and magazines, of which about half can only be grown well in outside pools or in conservatories. Some don't grow in water at all.

Many plants used in aquariums are not completely aquatic; here Echinodorus grandifolius, *one of the Amazon swordplants, is shown growing out of the water. Photo by H. Schultz.*

So if we search the world we could probably turn up a little over 200 usable aquarium plants, but less than 100 of these are generally offered for sale to the hobbyist.

Originally terrestrial

Most aquatic plants are descendants of plants that were originally terrestrial. Like a series of steps, there is a complete range from the perfect water plants, which have completely lost their ability to live on land, to the normal land-dwellers. In the middle there is a wide range of amphibious plants that are admirably adapted to living where water levels fluctuate greatly. They may be completely submerged for long periods and then adapt to a falling water level by changing their appearance completely and becoming land plants. Even though these plants become thoroughly adjusted to life on land, they never get far from water because they are unable to compete efficiently with the strictly terrestrial plants.

Nomenclature

These amphibious plants give a particularly hard time to the systematic botanists—those who name plants—because they are so variable and difficult to describe. Many of the amphibious plants have been given two or more names, one each for the very different land and water forms. Consider, for example, the extremes of the leaf types produced by a single cellophane swordplant. Submerged specimens may have nothing but strap-like leaves, while specimens growing out of water may have nothing but heart-shaped leaves.

Aquatic plants

While relatively few plants are strictly aquatic, some are so much so that they have lost their ability to produce roots. These include the hornworts (*Ceratophyllum*) and the bladderworts (*Utricularia*) with their tiny trapdoor pouches that catch little water animals and serve as nutrient absorbing organs. Many of the common bunch plants such as elodea, cabomba, hornwort, and *Hydrilla* are strictly aquatic, as are vallisneria, duckweeds, water lilies, and aponogeton.

Many of our most highly prized aquarium plants are amphibious, but they can live their whole lives without ever touching land or

Plants of the genus Utricularia *(wild-growing* Utricularia *species shown here) are among those that have no roots at all. Photo by T.J. Horeman.*

coming up above the surface of the water. The varieties of crypto-corynes, some of the swordplants, hygrophila, and water clover are good examples.

Land plants
How do water plants differ from land plants?

Most land plants have strengthening or stiffening structures that hold them erect, while water plants depend for support on the water they are immersed in. Land plants depend on a waxy cuticle covering the leaves and stems to keep them from drying out; water plants are in no danger of drying out and therefore don't need a cuticle. The intermediate or amphibious plants have a good cuticle when on land but only a trace when in water. Land plants are usually firm, compact, and dark green; water plants have an internal aerating system that makes them soft, spongy, and lighter green. Land plants are often hairy or spiny; water plants are smooth. The most specialized water plants have slender, tape-like, or finely cut leaves.

Some plants that are sold for aquariums do not fit the above generalizations, primarily because they are not in fact true aquatic plants.

Aquatic plants such as this Cryptocoryne pontederifolia *have less need than terrestrial plants for specialized structures to help hold their leaves erect. Photo by R. Zukal.*

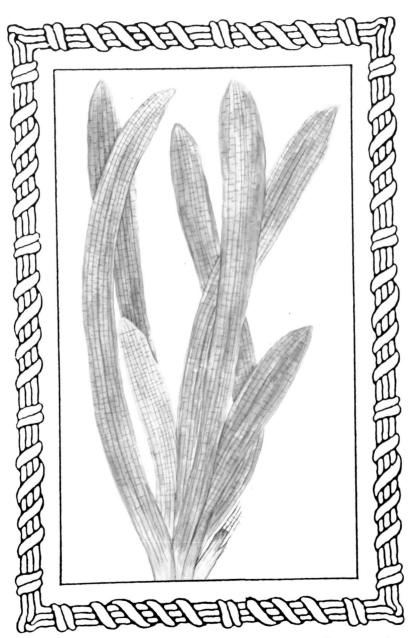

Sagittaria platyphylla *shows the typical light green coloration of many aquatic plants.*

Samolus floribundus, *sold under the name "water rose" but not a true aquatic.*

They should be considered temporary ornaments rather than permanent additions. Some of the little blue wild violets from your back yard will live for a time in your aquarium, but don't expect them to grow or open their flower buds. Other plants that will live but not grow are "water rose" (*Samolus floribundus*), "water orchid" (*Spiranthes*), and "Brazilian fern." The plants usually sold as "underwater pines" are club mosses (*Lycopodium* species, sometimes called ground pines). They are often collected in large quantities in rich old woods and dried for Christmas wreaths because they hold their color, do not shrivel, and look like miniature Christmas trees. There is nothing aquatic about these plants, though, and while they will hold up under water for a long time, they cannot grow in an aquarium.

Another interesting novelty is a very fine, plumy, delicate-looking but tough seaweed called coralline, which is collected in large quantities in certain warm ocean areas. It is a kind of red alga that retains its erect, delicate, feathery appearance when dried and deteriorates only slowly under water. It is often dyed various colors and sold under various trade names such as "Neptune fern," "color fern," or "aquafern."

16

2.
Requirements

Aquarium plants have the same basic requirements for normal growth as garden plants, with one important exception. In land plants, most of the details of structure are related to getting and keeping a favorable water balance, since water is one of the most important chemicals in the life of any organism. Water plants, however, normally have more water than they can use; if they have structures for procuring and storing water, these are simply carry-

Egeria densa, one of the popular "bunch" plants. Photo by R. Zukal.

Echinodorus longiscapus, *like most other plants of the genus* Echinodorus, *requires warm temperatures in order to do well. Photo by R. Zukal.*

overs from land-dwelling ancestors. Water plants depend on their environment for a constant water supply. If their homesite dries up, they simply shrivel away.

Temperature requirements

Most of our choicest aquarium plants are distinctly tropical and will not grow at low temperatures. The Amazon swordplant is an excellent example. At temperatures between 75 and 85°F. growth is rapid and new leaves are smooth and straight. Between 68 and 70°F. growth is still normal but slow. Between 60 and 65°F. not only is growth very slow, but the leaf veins mature before the leaf membranes, and as a result the leaves become puckered, narrower, and thicker. Below about 58°F. growth stops, and if the plants remain below this temperature for too long they will die. Examples of other warm-water plants are the varieties of cryptocorynes and water sprite.

Hardy plants that will thrive at low winter temperatures without heat include sagittaria, cabomba, hornwort, *Myriophyllum*, and Ludwigia.

Closeup of leaves of a Myriophyllum *species. Photo by William Tomey.*

At abnormally high temperatures (over 85°F.), plants require more light to maintain their vigor.

Light requirements

Scientists recognize a law of "limiting factors," which states that at any particular time the growth of a plant is limited by the one factor that is more inadequate than all the others. What this means is that you make a plant grow by repairing its worst deficiency of the moment.

If a plant has all the raw chemical material it can use and the temperature is at least 75°F. but the light is weak, then the limiting factor is light intensity; the plant will continue to grow faster as we increase the light intensity, up to a certain point. Beyond this point increased intensity will have no value.

Artificial light

The two chief sources of artificial light are incandescent, from a hot tungsten filament, and fluorescent, from an electric current passing through a gas-filled tube. Properly handled, either can give good aquarium illumination, but each has its limitations.

Flowers of Cabomba caroliniana; *aquarium plants won't flower unless their light requirements are met. Photo by T.J. Horeman.*

Aquarium reflectors available at pet shops are the best lighting devices available to the aquarist.

Incandescent light is richest in the warm colors yellow, orange, and red, so bright orange or red fishes such as some platies, swordtails, and guppies as well as glowlight tetras, serpae tetras, white clouds, and so on appear somewhat brighter under such light. On the other hand, while incandescent top lights are cheaper to purchase than fluorescent lights, they are much more expensive to operate.

The heat generated by the light source may be another critical factor. An incandescent top light generates several times as much heat as a fluorescent one. If the water in the aquarium is circulated by aeration or a filter and the air temperature of the room is moderate, this heat won't matter much unless too large a bulb is used (or if the light is burned too long) over a small covered aquarium. But during the summer, in non air-conditioned rooms, the additional heat may be disastrous.

Rooting medium

Most aquarium gravels now on the market are quite satisfactory, and nothing need be added to give good root and plant growth. A grain size of 1/16 to 1/8 inch is usually most desirable. It may be

Elodea nuttalli, *a plant that can do well in hard water.*
Photo by R. Zukal.

pure quartz or screened crushed granite. Milk-white flaky grits are crushed marble and are less desirable because they tend to dissolve in the water, making it too hard for some plants and fishes. Beautiful aquariums have been kept even with marble gravel, but the owners had to change one fourth of the water every two weeks and use lime-tolerant plants such as vallisneria, ambulia, *Hydrilla*, and *Elodea*.

3.
Enemies

If you have provided for all the above requirements and your plants still do not have the lush appearance you are striving for, you should consider the following as possible reasons for their failure to thrive:

Browsers
There are many fishes that eat plants faster than they can grow, and

Beautiful greenery provided by a lush growth of Cabomba caroliniana. *Photo by Burkhard Kahl.*

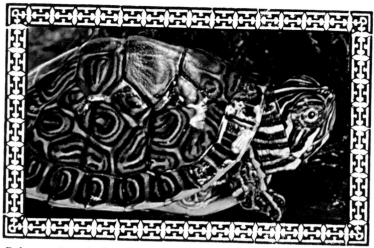

Baby aquatic turtles kept in a planted aquarium will soon bite holes in the soft leaves of aquarium plants. Photo by Dr. Herbert R. Axelrod.

the more delectable plants can't possibly be grown in the company of such fishes. A number of characins (tetra family) are offenders along this line. *Metynnis*, scats, and *Abramites* will eat anything green (plus some things that aren't even very green). While they are less likely to do damage, other characins with a tendency to pick on plants at times include *Moenkhausia*, *Hemiodus*, *Ctenobrycon*, and at times serpae tetras and blind cave characins. Botias may disfigure broad-leaved plants like swordplants, crypts, and aponogetons by popping paper-punch-like holes through the younger leaves. They may virtually eat the heart out of swordplants. Angelfish at spawning time may suck holes in swordplants while cleaning off leaves to be used as spawning sites. The various strains of *Poecilia sphenops* mollies have lips that are well covered with fine, sharp teeth. As they busily use these to scrape algae and tiny animals off plants, they may give the leaves a worn, sandpapered appearance.

Snails

Under certain circumstances, snails may browse on plants. In particular, the giant Florida apple snail, *Pomacea paludosa* is such a destructive feeder on aquatic plants that it should not be kept in an aquarium. This snail is sometimes sold as the "nursemaid" or "infusoria snail," to be housed in a separate tank or jar and fed generously on lettuce or water plants. Its decomposing droppings sup-

24

Crayfish such as this egg-carrying female will make short work of most aquarium plants that can be snipped off near the bottom. Photo by J. Elias.

port a rich protozoan culture, which provides a first food for baby fish. Interestingly, a close relative of this snail, *Pomacea bridgesi*, the "mystery snail," eats aquarium plants only as a last resort, when there is a shortage of other foods. Aquarium snails have a sort of food preference list. If a variety of foods is available they will first choose dead fish or almost any prepared food. Mystery snails are fond of whiteworms. Next they will eat algae and tiny animals that cover plants, rocks, and the sides of the aquarium. If these foods are inadequate they will turn on the ornamental plants, choosing first such soft things as water sprite, ambulia, or hygrophila. Eventually they may even eat young swordplant leaves.

Snails can perform valuable services as scavengers and polishers if they can be kept from becoming so abundant that competition forces them to eat the plants. If this happens several remedies may be used. You may pick out as many snails as possible by hand and throw them away. You may float a partially wilted lettuce leaf in the aquarium as bait, lift it out with a net when it is well covered with snails, shake the snails off, return the leaf, and repeat the pro-

"Mystery" snails are not actively predacious on aquarium plants unless they're forced into it by lack of other suitable foods.

Geophagus jurupari is one of the most active of the substrate-shifting fish species. Photo by H. Hansen.

cess each day until most of the snails are removed. You can use gold barbs, blue gouramis, or baby turtles, which are effective snail eradicators.

But the simplest method of getting rid of unwanted snails is to poison them. There are several types of snail eradicators available. Those based on copper are more toxic to the aquarium plants. You can get a specific formula from your dealer to do the job. Just follow the instructions.

Excavators
Another class of plant enemies that may damage plants without actually eating them includes chiefly the larger cichlids such as Jack Dempseys, acaras, *Astronotus*, and chanchito. These fishes are so active in shifting gravel around that it is quite impossible to maintain healthy rooted plants with them unless the space between the plants is well covered with boulders. Large plecostomus catfishes (*Hypostomus*) may also dig vigorously.

The substrate in which this Samolus valerandi *is planted is just about the correct degree of coarseness, neither too fine and densely packed nor too coarse. Photo by R. Zukal.*

Keep it clean

Excess food lodging in the plant crowns can cause problems. But overfeeding, with its tendency to pollute the gravel, is a more general problem. Before filtration came into general use, overfeeding resulted in a cloudy tank. Today's filters remove the cloud and reduce the effects of mismanagement, but if the excess is gross the mechanical system cannot remove the source and the result is black gravel.

Undergravel or biological filters are particularly valuable in these cases, but they too have their limitations. The gravel turns black below the surface—best seen where the gravel extends above the edge of the frame. The plant roots too turn black and slimy, and frequently the entire crown breaks loose from the base. Bunch plants shed their leaves, while rooted plants lose their color.

Prevention is best, but if the condition is well advanced the only remedy is to replace the gravel—don't wash the old but throw it out, unless you can sun bleach it.

Uneaten fish food should not be allowed to accumulate around the crowns of the plants, as it could cause the plants to rot at their bases; the healthy Valllisneria americana *shown here have their substrate properly free of debris. Photo by T.J. Horeman.*

Aponogeton ulvaceus *flowering under greenhouse cultivation. Photo by T. J. Horeman.*

"Transplanters"

One of the greatest enemies of aquarium plants is the transplanter, the aquarist who decides each week that things just don't look right, proceeds to move the plants about, makes other changes, and occasionally tears the whole aquarium down and starts over. He never allows the plants to become established. Some of the finest plants—*Cryptocoryne*, for example—thrive only if their roots are not disturbed.

Overfeeding

When excessive amounts of dried foods are introduced into an aquarium the surplus becomes waterlogged and, sinking to the bottom, frequently finds lodgment among the roots of the plants. As it slowly decomposes, the fermentation products extend to the leaf stems, which turn brown at the contact area—the base—and rot through, eventually breaking loose. The leaf appears healthy except at the base, which is often slimy or pulpy.

4.
Propagation

Most of the more desirable aquarium plants may be propagated in the aquarium. Some reproduce freely without aid from the aquarist, but others will do better with some assistance.

Reproduction is either by sexual means, involving flowers and seed formation, or asexual, sometimes called vegetative propagation. Aquatic plants tend to favor asexual means; only a few depend on seeds as their chief means of reproduction.

Echinodorus magdalensis *growing in a nutrient-rich basket designed for aquarium use; this obviously healthy specimen has produced young plants attached to a "runner." Photo by Edward C. Taylor.*

Flowers and seeds of Aponogeton fenestratus. *Photo by T.J. Horeman.*

Seed formation

The only popular aquarium plants that can be depended upon to produce viable seeds in aquariums are the various species of *Aponogeton*, and these produce specialized aquatic seeds that would be quite unsatisfactory for land plants. Aponogeton seeds at maturity are large and bright green, about like small green peas, but naked, since the delicate seed coats disintegrate as the seeds mature. They sprout immediately into robust seedlings. Most land-plant seeds have tough coats that protect the embryo from injury and drying; they usually lie dormant for a period before germinating.

Some other aquarium plants are commonly propagated by seeds produced under natural pond conditions. Among these are cellophane swordplants and spatterdocks.

A number of plants flower quite readily in aquariums but rarely produce good seed. These include cryptocorynes, sagittaria, swordplants, vallisneria, elodea, and hornwort.

Cuttings

Virtually all aquatics with small leaves attached to long, slender stems can be propagated by cuttings. If a tall shoot is cut near the middle and the cut end of the upper half is pushed into the gravel it will promptly produce roots. The old plant base will suddenly send out a group of new shoots producing a prettier bush clump. This process can be repeated over and over to produce great numbers of plants. Hygrophila, ludwigia, ambulia, water wisteria, temple plants, *Cabomba*, and *Myriophyllum* can be handled in this way and sprout at every joint. Elodea behaves similarly but can produce roots and branches only at every eighth or ninth joint.

Crown division

The so-called "stemless" plants that produce a rosette of leaves from a central crown include most of the choicest aquarium plants—swordplants, cryptocorynes, lace plants, and aquarium lilies. These plants are of great value, and some do not propagate in

Hygrophila polysperma, *one of the many aquarium plants that can be reproduced from cuttings. Photo by T.J. Horeman.*

Cryptocoryne beckettii, *capable of being propagated through crown division. Photo by T.J. Horeman.*

aquariums by any other means or propagate only slowly. Separation of a large crown into two or more smaller ones is a practical method of propagating these plants, but it requires a basic understanding of the structure of compound plant crowns to be practiced successfully.

Most plant stems are made up of joints, called nodes, separated by longer bare segments, called internodes. All leaves and buds and most new roots come from the nodes. The so-called stemless plants actually lack only the internode development. They have very compact stems that do not grow tall because the short nodes are joined closely one to another like a stack of coins. It is better to call them rosette plants, because the very abbreviated stems hold the leaves in compact rosettes.

These plants produce branches just like erect growing plants, and each branch forms a new rosette alongside the parent one. Unless a plant crown includes two or more rosettes it cannot be divided, no matter how large it is or how many leaves it has. As you look down into a large plant from above, the number of rosettes will be re-

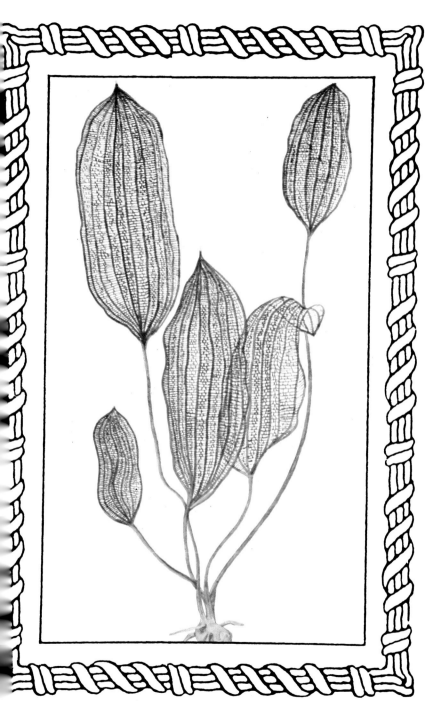

Aponogeton henkelianus, *a lace plant, has crown division as only one of its methods of reproduction.*

vealed by the number of growing points from which new leaves are arising, and that tells how many smaller plants you can divide the large plant into.

To be successful, a crown division must include several well-developed leaves firmly attached to an ample stem segment and preferably with some of its own roots. Don't be too hasty in removing a young rosette or you will have a handful of worthless leaves and no plant. Be patient until the young rosette has a good many leaves and is flourishing; then carefully sort the leaves so your fingers encircle all those belonging to the young shoot and no more. Slide your fingers as deeply into the crown as possible and slowly roll the young rosette back and out from the parent until it breaks free. Then shake it back and forth to free it from the gravel as you pull it out. If a large clump is to be completely split up, it is easier and faster to lift the entire clump.

A large robust plant that shows no tendency to produce offshoots can be prompted to do so by a simple operation. Slide a long, slen-

Echinodorus peruensis *with flower stalk bearing young plants. Photo by Edward C. Taylor.*

Closeup of a flower stalk and young plants produced by the swordplant Echinodorus osiris. *Photo by R. Zukal.*

der screwdriver or some similar object down beside the youngest leaf until you meet the firm stem, and twist the screwdriver. That will usually dislodge a young leaf or two and injure the growing point. The plant will respond by producing several side shoots just like a tall plant that has its top removed.

Runners or stolons
Some plants produce slender horizontal branches that creep along the soil or burrow through it. These creeping branches end in young plants that usually develop rapidly as long as they remain attached to the parent plant but are severely set back if they are separated too soon. Plants with several large leaves and good root development may safely be separated if necessary.

This is the chief means of propagation of the grass-like sagittaria and vallisneria. Each young plant promptly sends out another runner, resulting in a long chain of plants, each a little smaller than the

Vallisneria asiatica *normally reproduces in the aquarium by production of runners.*

last, leading away from the parent plant. While these plants also produce crown divisions, they mostly rely on their runners to produce new plants.

All true *Cryptocoryne* species produce runners, as do some swordplants and even ambulia. Some swordplant "runners" are actually flowering stalks. In bright light these may be rigid, projecting above the water and producing at least three white flowers at each joint. Some swordplants produce mostly long slender flower stalks that remain beneath the water surface. The flower buds on these usually do not open normally. These stalks are an excellent illustration of the next type of propagation.

Livebearing plants
Each joint of a submerged swordplant flower stalk bears three slender scale leaves. Above each is a flower bud, and from the attachment of each bud arises a complete baby plant, three plants per joint.

When the leaves and roots of a new plant are well developed, hold it between your thumb and index finger at the base and hold the runner firmly with your other hand on the side away from the par-

Cryptocoryne bullosa *showing the plant's odd leaf structure. Photo by T. J. Horeman.*

ent. Press the shoot back along the runner toward the parent, rocking it as you apply pressure. If you do this carefully, the young plant will break free without injury to the runner and may be planted where you like. Several aquatic plants produce perfect miniatures of themselves on their mature leaves. The most notable of these are certain tropical water lilies, water bananas (*Nymphoides*), and water ferns (*Ceratopteris*). The livebearing faculty is occasionally demonstrated to a remarkable degree by the tropical lilies. The young plants that develop in the notches of the floating leaves may be so vigorous, under favorable conditions, that they produce roots and miniature flowers of their own while still firmly attached to the middle of a large lily pad. The floating water ferns and water sprites produce a great profusion of young plants, one from every leaf notch, and they are such persistent livebearers that it is not uncommon to find three or even four generations joined together: we may find tiny new plants on the leaves of somewhat larger young plants that already have roots but are attached to larger plants that may in turn be still attached to large old plants that are turning brown as they ripen off and produce spores.

Water bananas produce a cluster of flowers from a swelling near the top of the leaf stalk, just beneath the floating pad. At the same point a cluster of thick, fleshy, green banana-like roots is produced and soon followed by the young leaves of a new plant.

Hygrophila produces young plants from the base of any detached leaf, as do several other aquatic plants.

Fragmentation
Under certain conditions elodea and a few other plants develop weak spots at regular intervals of every eighth or ninth joint. Any strong water current will then break up the long shoot into as many fragments as there are weak spots, and each fragment can produce just one set of new shoots and roots.

Winter buds (turions)
Some hardy aquatics can be grown from special dormant winter buds that sink to the bottoms of ponds in the fall and sprout in the spring or when moved to a warm aquarium. Among these plants are bladderworts, pondweeds (*Potamogeton*), duckweeds, and *Myriophyllum*. The lotus produces huge yellow banana-like overwintering structures.

5.
Selection

A hardy half dozen

To simplify the selection of aquarium plants while you are becoming familiar with the wide variety available, I recommend almost any combination of the following six handsome, easily grown types. They all tolerate a wide variety of water conditions, moderate to strong light, and small to large aquariums, and they all propagate freely without aid.

Cryptocoryne affinis, *unquestionably among the very best suited to aquarium life of all* Cryptocoryne *species. Photo by R. Zukal.*

Water sprite (Ceratopteris) *is prolific whether kept as a rooted plant or a floating plant. Photo courtesy Dr. D. Terver, Nancy Aquarium.*

Prolific Crypt (*Cryptocoryne affinis*): It grows 6 to 16 inches long, depending on light and aquarium size. The leaves are velvety blue-green above and wine red below. This large and graceful plant is by far the fastest growing and most prolific member of this aristocratic group.

Water Sprite (*Ceratopteris thalicroides*), Broad or Narrow varieties: This is a true fern with beautiful light green, deeply cut fronds that can grow a foot long. It is extremely fast growing and propagating. Discard old plants from time to time and replace them with young offshoots. Water sprite grows well, rooted or floating. It furnishes excellent cover for baby fish, which makes it a favorite with breeders of fancy guppies. Protect it from plant-eating fish and snails.

Hygrophila (*Hygrophila*): The best leafy-stemmed plant, it resembles ludwigia but requires less light and grows faster.

Narrow Sagittaria (*Sagittaria subulata*): There are several varieties. It forms a rich green grass from 3 to 12 inches high. It grows well in cool or warm aquariums with good light and makes graceful end thickets.

Corkscrew Vallisneria (*Vallisneria spiralis*): This plant makes pretty light-green twisted grassy leaves. It should not be shaded; it likes side light and water that is not too soft.

42

Giant Hornwort (*Ceratophyllum* species): This plant, which looks like slender pine branches spreading freely beneath the water surface, is a graceful addition to the decor as well as a valuable hiding place for eggs, baby fish, and shy, slow-moving, or injured fishes. The needle-like leaves intercept so little of the light that they give practically no interference to the rooted plants growing beneath. The hornworts are so utterly aquatic they have lost the ability to produce functional roots, they never rise above the surface, and even their tiny flowers open and produce seeds entirely underwater.

While the plant looks delicate, it is seldom damaged by snails or plant-eating fishes, and if it is broken into fragments each fragment continues to grow.

The common hornwort is a fair substitute for the giant species, but it casts a denser shade. If you collect it from a limewater pond it will shed badly when first introduced.

The harsh hornwort is not very satisfactory; it sheds badly, appears stunted, and is too stiff and rough to be attractive.

Three hornwort varieties: harsh hornwort (smallest plants), common hornwort (medium-size plants), giant hornwort (largest plants). Photo by Dr. D. Jacobs.

Given good light and water quality, Vallisneria *will soon carpet the bottom of an aquarium with attractive greenery. Photo by G. Wolfsheimer.*

Hobbyists often have access to other good aquarium plants besides those already described; in fact, some desirable plants often are in better supply than the "big six." Following are descriptions of a few of these other plants, which make good subjects for experimentation by aquarists and are desirable in their own right, not just as fill-ins for more popular species.

Liverworts and mosses
These lowly spore-bearing plants grow in damp places all over the world, but only one common liverwort, *Riccia*, and a few mosses have been widely used in aquariums.

Riccia fluitans (crystalwort) and a few close relatives grow in pretty bright green tufts floating just beneath the surface. They are used for the shelter of young livebearers and to receive the spawn of some varieties of tetras and killifishes. *Riccia* may inferfere with the growth of rooted aquarium plants if you let it cover the aquarium completely. It does not thrive in soft water.

Fontinalis or willow mosses grow attached to rocks in fast streams. Because they are tough and do not deteriorate rapidly, they are

Riccia fluitans, *a floating plant that provides good shelter for top-dwelling fishes and is often used to anchor nests of gouramis and bettas. Photo by R. Zukal.*

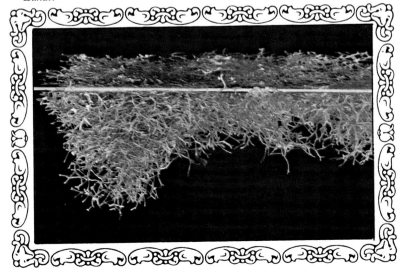

used as spawn receivers, but they do not grow well in aquariums and so are not regarded as permanent additions.

Vesicularia, Java moss, is a true aquatic that grows quite rapidly into lacy, bright green thickets with brown spore capsules.

Water Clover (*Marsilea*): This includes several species of unusual plants, relatives of the ferns, with four-leaf clover leaves that unroll like fern fronds. They come to us from Europe, Asia, and Australia, and are also found in our own country.

These are very desirable, sturdy ground-cover plants. To keep them growing low and compactly, avoid overhanging plants and supply good top light, preferably fluorescent. Additional daylight coming in the front will also help. Branching and compactness can be encouraged further by clipping rapidly growing runners behind the third or fourth leaf. Water clover is particularly resistant to drugs and tolerates most water conditions, including wide ranges of temperature, pH, and hardness.
To propagate this plant, cut up the long runners, leaving at least four leaves to each section. The pill-like spore capsules are produced only on emergent plants growing under strong light in shal-

Marsilea quadrifolia *growing in emersed form. Photo by R. Zukal.*

46

Java moss, Vesicularia dubyana.

low water and are of no use for propagating the plant in an aquarium. In some Australian lowlands where Water Clovers are abundant, the sporangia are gathered and beaten into a sort of hard bread by the aborigines, who call the plant Nardoo.

Flowering Plants

Family ALISMATACEAE
Echinodorus quadricostatus (**Dwarf Amazon Sword**): Also commonly referred to as *E. intermedius*, this small species hails from the Amazon. Very easy to grow, it will quickly cover the floor of the tank with plants. The leaves are similar in color and shape to its larger brethren, but reach only about four inches long. If you want this plant as a single or just a small clump, then pinch off the runners as they appear. Because of the soft nature of the leaves, it must be handled with care. Rooted.

Echinodorus bleheri (**Amazon Swordplant**): This magnificent plant can grow to a height of 20 inches and form a beautiful eye-catching centerpiece in any tank large enough to accommodate its size. The translucent green leaves resemble lances protruding from the gravel. The plant propagates itself by sending out floating runners from the crown with new plants forming at intervals; these put out side-shoots which soon root in the compost. It likes moderate top lighting and should be left undisturbed after planting. Its leaves are often brittle and snap easily; because the leaf later rots at the break, remove a broken leaf at the crown. A fair amount of feeding is needed if the swordplant is to attain its maximum growth. It can reproduce by throwing up short stems capped by white flowers, though this is not a common occurrence in the home aquarium.

Excess dry fish food falling into the crown may rot there, and the mold will affect the leaf. Overfeeding may also result in polluted gravel which, in addition to other problems, can cause a rotting at the base of rooted plants.

If your tank is on the small side and thus unsuitable for the giant growth of this swordplant, then try *Echinodorus amazonicus*. The leaves of this sword only grow to about 8 inches. Water a little on the soft side and careful feeding will soon have this junior Amazon flourishing.

The Amazon swordplant Echinodorus bleheri. *Photo by R. Zukal.*

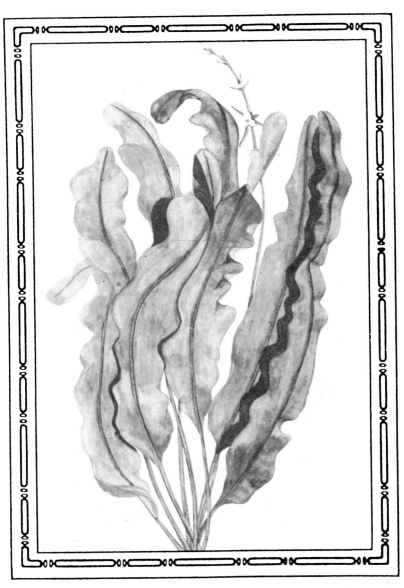

Echinodorus martii; *note the delicate white flowers on the stalk.*

Family APONOGETONACEAE

Aponogeton madagascariensis (**Madagascar Lace Plant**): This plant was once considered the status symbol of the "In" aquarium. Its large leaves, ovate in shape, are pierced, giving a skeleton-like appearance. Though these leaves look fragile, they are, in fact, quite tough. Unless snails are kept in the aquarium, the interstices of the leaves soon become blocked with algal growth. Not easy to cultivate in the home aquarium. Best purchased as a young plant or as a tuber. Rooted.

Aponogeton crispus: This is one of the most common of this large group of plants. It does best in slightly acid waters, and when conditions are right will tower to a height of 18 inches. Its habitat is Sri Lanka. The large, crinkly-edged leaves are found in various shades of green.

Family HALORAGACEAE

Myriophyllum hippuroides (**Water Milfoil, Foxtail**): Unless this plant receives good light, the long spiky leaves break off. Don't use

Closeup of Myriophyllum hippuroides, *showing the bushy delicacy of the leaves. Photo by R. Zukal.*

Ludwigia natans. *Photo by T. J. Horeman.*

floating plants that shade an aquarium containing milfoil. Native to most of the United States, though usually green in color it is also available in red. It is excellent for hiding the fry of livebearers and receiving the spawn of egglayers. Bunch plant.

Family HYDROCHARITACEA

Elodea densa (**Canadian Pond Weed, Elodea**): Dark green whorls on long-growing stems that must have plenty of illumination; otherwise, the lanceolate leaves turn brown and the plant rots away. It will tolerate hard water and is not very fussy over conditions. Planted in bunches, the stems are fastened together and buried just below the gravel. A coarse form, *E. crispa*, is more suitable for growth at low temperatures. Bunch plant. Often put in the genus *Egeria* and also called anacharis.

Family NYMPHAEACEAE

Cabomba caroliniana (**Cabomba**): This plant is similar in appearance to ambulia but is a bright green. The fronds grow paired on opposite sides of the central stem (the fronds of ambulia grow all around). Allow the cuttings to float for a short time before planting. Though considered a bunch plant, it grows better planted singly than in groups. It likes cool, lime-free, soft water. It has at least

51

Kept in water that is too warm, these lovely strands of Cabomba caroliniana *would soon become stringy. Photo by R. Zukal.*

An emersed form of Bacopa amplexicaulis. *Photo by T. J. Horeman.*

six different leaf forms. The end of each stem forms thick crowns under the water surface; give strong top light.

Family ONAGRACEAE
Ludwigia natans (**Ludwigia**): This is a South American bog plant with lance-like leaves, dark green on the surface and reddish tinged underneath. There is also a red-leaved variety, as well as a rounded leaf form. The red extends into the stems as pink. Bunch plant.

Ludwigia likes to grow above the water, and if left unchecked in the aquarium it will grow right out of the tank. If conditions aren't suitable, the leaves will turn brown and fall off. It prefers soft water conditions and strong top light.

Family SCROPHULARIACEAE
Bacopa caroliniana (**Water Hyssop, Baby's Tears**): This plant has small oval leaves, leathery in texture, that protrude nearly horizontally from long, round stems. The fleshy green leaves are sometimes tinged with red or brown. Best planted in clumps; if given partial shade it will produce rich growth after emerging above the water. It is not popular with professional growers because of its

53

slow growth. The leaves have a distinctive spearmint odor out of the water. In Europe, it is commonly called Baby's Tears. Bunch plant.

Limnophila sessiliflora (**Ambulia**): With its divided leaves in whorls, this is a quick prolific grower if given good, strong top light. It is usually purchased without roots, but these quickly form in the tank. Its habitat is Ceylon, India, and parts of Africa. It grows to 15 inches. If kept under natural light only, it dies back in the winter months. Often referred to the genus *Ambulia*. Bunch plant.

Artificial Plants

Despite the fact that the mere mention of "artificial" foliage will draw sighs of protest from many plant growers and aquarists, imitation plants are popular throughout the world. Reasonable in price and with a wide variety of shapes, sizes, and colors to choose from, they have many things to commend their use to the fishkeeper. Made for the most part of pressed plastic, they discourage the growth of snail populations. Unlike living plants, they cannot be

Certain aquarium plants, Fontinalis *and* Vesicularia *especially, can be combined nicely with pieces of driftwood and other natural decorations to create attractive vistas. Shown is* Vesicularia dubyana. *Photo by R. Zukal.*

Limnophila sessiliflora, *usually sold under the common name ambulia, is a highly decorative plant. Photo by R. Zukal.*

eaten or damaged by the attentions of snails and fishes. Should disease strike the tank, they can be quickly removed and sterilized without any fuss. Interspersed between natural plants, they can add color and shape.

Aquarium plants available to the hobbyist are not usually what one would call colorful. Their foliage varies between the shades of green, red, and purple. Artificial plants, on the other hand, can be obtained in almost any color one desires and, if realism isn't essential, they fit the bill of decoration admirably. The majority on sale are non-toxic, but if you do purchase any from a source other than an aquarium dealer, check before adding them to the aquarium. Immersion for a few days with a few live daphnia will soon tell you. After prolonged immersion in the aquarium, they do become covered with natural growth, especially algae. A good brushing with a stiff brush and a rinsing under the faucet are all that is required to restore their original coloration. Like most soft plastic, they fade and become brittle after long immersion, but they are generally so inexpensive that it is simple to replace them.

Artificial aquarium plants available today are great improvements over the ones marketed years ago; they're much more lifelike. **Opposite:** *Artificial plants can be artistically combined with other types of aquarium ornamentation to provide very pleasing effects. Photo by Vincent Serbin.*

A sprig of water wisteria is here being weighted down with a rock. Water wisteria will grow well whether planted in the gravel or left to float freely. Photo by R. Zukal.

6.
Planting

Compared to dirt gardening, there are very few rules or precautions to observe when planting aquarium plants. Many aquatic plants are obtained as rootless cuttings that root promptly after having their cut ends pushed into the gravel. Rooted plants should be prepared by pulling off damaged roots and other discolored leaves before planting. Outer leaves should always be removed by pulling downward toward roots and peeling sideways. Extremely long roots

Aquarium stores offer a wide selection of devices that can be useful in handling planting chores; such items are particularly useful in deep tanks.

should be clipped to 2 inches or less in length. Gather roots neatly between thumb and first two fingers and push into sand using index finger to push and thumb and middle finger to cover roots.

After selecting the plants to be used they may be arranged in any manner that pleases you but certain principles will be worth keeping in mind:

(1) Keep dwarf plants and plants that require strong light in the more open, forward, and higher locations.

(2) Plant tall or rank growing types at the sides or back.

(3) Use plants with brightly colored leaves (red-leaved crypts) as accents in prominent places.

(4) Plant water sprite, banana plants, aquarium lilies, etc., directly over undergravel filters since those thrive over such filters.

(5) Do not cover the entire bottom of the aquarium with an undergravel filter. Half is enough.

(6) Plant in small groups rather than scattered hit or miss.

(7) Use rocks to help set off specimen plants.

(8) Use tall plants to conceal heaters, filters, etc.

Echinodorus aschersonianus. *Photo by R. Zukal.*

Suggested Reading

The following books, available at pet shops and bookstores everywhere, contain additional information of interest and value to anyone wishing to learn about aquarium plants.

LIGHT IN THE AQUARIUM
By Rolf Kubler
ISBN 0-87666-096-0
TFH PS-301

Contents: The Metric System. The "Problem Child" Aquarium. Looking At Light From A Physical Aspect. Light And Plants. Measuring The Luminous Intensity. Daylight Or Artificial Light. Artificial Light. Reciprocal Effect Of Plant-Light-Water.

Audience: This text is written for the hobbyist who perhaps does not realize the importance of light in keeping fish healthy. The chapters cover such areas as: photosynthesis, light and growth, direct measurements, luminous intensity by artificial light, and fluorescent lamps. High school graduates and above.

Soft cover; 8 x 5½; 96 pp.
25 black and white photos; 25 color photos; 19 line illustrations.

AQUARIUM PLANTS
By Dr. K. Rataj and T. Horeman
ISBN 0-87666-455-9
TFH H-966

Contents: General Principles For The Cultivation Of Aquatic Plants. Illumination Of The Aquarium. Fully Aquatic And Amphibious Plants In Nature And The Aquarium. Algae In The Aquarium. Reproduction In Aquatic Plants. Practical Propagation Of Aquarium Plants. Characteristics Of Tropical Floral Areas. Non-Flowering Plants. Flowering Plants. Identification Keys.

Audience: Designed for use by aquarium hobbyists, horticulturists, botanists and students, this massive and very highly colorful book is the most complete volume ever published about aquarium plants. High school level.

Hard cover; 5½ x 8; 448 pp.
244 color photos, 124 black and white photos.